BLACK TRAILBLAZERS IN SPORTS

BILL RUSSELL

by David Lee Morgan Jr.

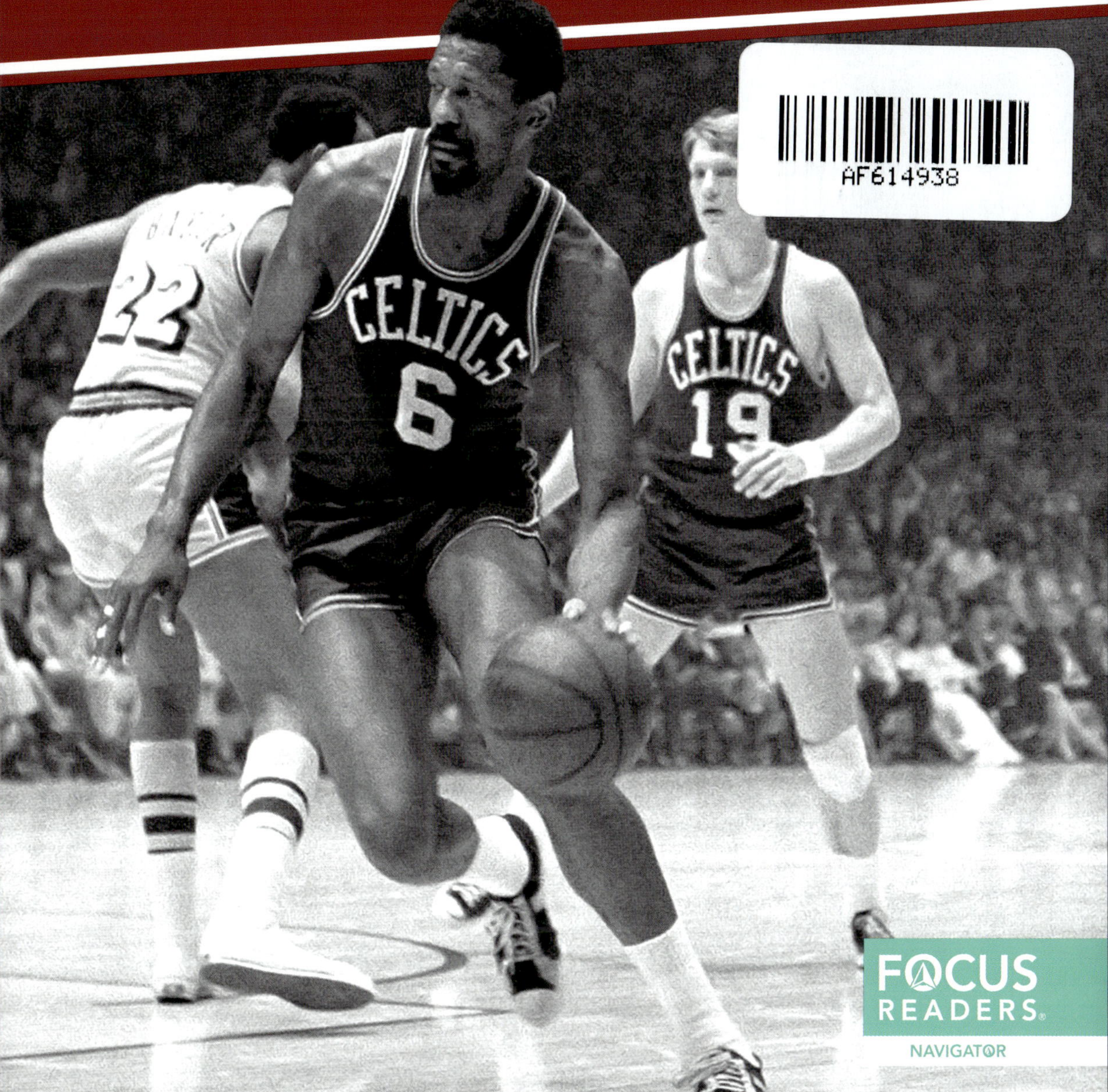

FOCUS READERS

NAVIGATOR

WWW.FOCUSREADERS.COM

Focus Readers is distributed by North Star Editions:
sales@northstareditions.com | 888-417-0195

Produced for Focus Readers by Red Line Editorial.

Photographs ©: Harold P. Matosian/AP Images, cover, 1; Richard Meek/Sports Illustrated/Getty Images, 4–5, 6; Bettmann/Getty Images, 9, 15, 16–17, 19; Marion Post Wolcott/New York Public Library, 10–11; William Straeter/AP Images, 13; Tony Tomsic/AP Images, 21; AP Images, 22–23; Chip Somodevilla/Getty Images News/Getty Images, 25; Marcio Jose Sanchez/AP Images, 27; Red Line Editorial, 29

Library of Congress Cataloging-in-Publication Data
Names: Morgan, David Lee, author.
Title: Bill Russell / by David Lee Morgan Jr.
Description: Mendota Heights, MN: Focus Readers, [2025] | Series: Black trailblazers in sports | Includes bibliographical references and index. | Audience: Grades 4-6
Identifiers: LCCN 2024000669 (print) | LCCN 2024000670 (ebook) | ISBN 9798889982135 (hardcover) | ISBN 9798889982692 (paperback) | ISBN 9798889983767 (pdf) | ISBN 9798889983255 (ebook)
Subjects: LCSH: Russell, Bill 1934-2022--Juvenile literature. | Basketball players--United States--Biography--Juvenile liteature. | African American basketball players--Biography--Juvenile literature.
Classification: LCC GV884.R86 M67 2025 (print) | LCC GV884.R86 (ebook) | DDC 796.323092 [B]--dc23/eng/20240111
LC record available at https://lccn.loc.gov/2024000669
LC ebook record available at https://lccn.loc.gov/2024000670

Printed in the United States of America
Mankato, MN
082024

ABOUT THE AUTHOR

David Lee Morgan Jr. is the author of 11 books, including *LeBron James: The Rise of a Star* and *Breaking Through the Lines: The Marion Motley Story*. Morgan was a longtime sportswriter with the *Akron Beacon Journal* and is now a high school English teacher and public speaker.

TABLE OF CONTENTS

CHAPTER 1

The 1957 Finals 5

CHAPTER 2

A College Great 11

CHAPTER 3

Becoming a Legend 17

CHAPTER 4

Large Legacy 23

At-a-Glance Map • 28

Focus on Bill Russell • 30

Glossary • 31

To Learn More • 32

Index • 32

HAWKS
9
ELTICS
6
HAWKS
22
14
6

CHAPTER 1

THE 1957 FINALS

Bill Russell stepped onto the court. The **rookie** center was about to make a name for himself. He and the Boston Celtics were playing in the 1957 Finals. They faced the St. Louis Hawks. Both teams had already won three games in the series. So, Game 7 would decide the champion of the National Basketball

Bill Russell (6) contests a rebound during the 1957 NBA Finals.

The 1957 Finals were close. Four of the seven games were decided by two points.

Association (NBA). Game 7 was close from start to finish. St. Louis led 53–51 at halftime. But Boston entered the fourth quarter up 83–77. From there, the game went back and forth.

Less than a minute remained in the fourth quarter. Russell powered his way toward the basket and scored. He put Boston up 102–101. Then St. Louis moved the ball up the court on a breakaway. Hawks forward Jack Coleman attempted a layup. But Russell swatted the ball away, making an incredible **chase-down block**. Thanks to Russell's play, Boston remained in the lead. The Celtics made one free throw. Then the Hawks managed to tie it. The game went into **overtime**.

When the extra period ended, the score was tied at 113. So, the game went into a second overtime. This time, the Celtics pulled ahead in the closing seconds. Boston won 125–123. The hometown crowd poured onto the court in celebration. It was Boston's first-ever NBA championship.

Russell finished with 19 points. Plus, he had nabbed 32 rebounds. That was an amazing feat for a rookie. But most people talked about Russell's block.

THE BLOCK

Russell played during a time when blocks weren't an official NBA statistic. So, no one knows exactly how many he racked up. But he was one of the best shot blockers ever. Russell used blocks to start fast breaks. A fast break is when an offense tries to score before defenders have time to run back. Fast breaks left the Celtics with many easy layups.

Boston coach Red Auerbach (left) and forward Tom Heinsohn celebrate their 1957 Finals victory.

A teammate said it was one of the most memorable plays he'd ever seen. In his first year in the NBA, Russell had won a championship ring. It was the first of many more to come.

CHAPTER 2

A COLLEGE GREAT

Bill Russell was born on February 12, 1934, in Monroe, Louisiana. His family faced racism in the **segregated** South. **Discrimination** made it hard for his father to find good work. As a result, the family moved when Bill was eight years old. They went to Oakland, California. They hoped for better opportunities there. Many other

Housing for enslaved Black Americans remained standing through the 1900s. Racist systems did, too. These systems led to the Great Migration.

Black Americans left the South during this period. It became known as the Great Migration.

Bill's mother died when he was 12. After she died, Bill became shy. He started spending hours at the library. Bill fell in love with reading. He developed a sharp mind. Later, it would help him rethink how basketball could be played.

Bill was already 5-foot-10 (178 cm) in his first year of high school. He made the basketball team easily. He was not skilled, but he learned. He also kept growing. By his final year, he stood 6-foot-5 (196 cm).

However, no major colleges wanted Russell. Only the University of San

Russell often led his college basketball team in rebounds and points.

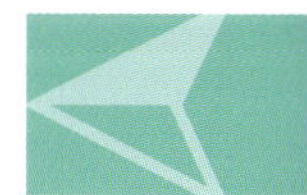

Francisco showed an interest. And the San Francisco Dons didn't have a great basketball team. That changed when Russell arrived in 1952. In the 1954–55 season, San Francisco lost just one game all season. Russell led the Dons to a championship.

Russell and his team faced racism. For example, they played in Oklahoma City, Oklahoma, in 1954. The hotels there would not rent rooms to the Black players. The team stuck together, though. They all stayed in an empty dorm.

PASSED OVER

Russell experienced many kinds of racism in college. In 1955, his team had just won the national title. He was named Most Outstanding Player of the Final Four. Russell was also a first-team All-American. But he wasn't picked as the best college player in Northern California. A white player was picked instead.

Russell changed how basketball players defended. He was one of the first players to make jumping shot blocks.

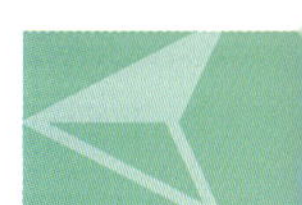

Russell continued to improve his game. His final college season was his best yet. This time, the Dons didn't lose a single game. They won their second title in a row.

6
JAPAN
7
8
3

CHAPTER 3

BECOMING A LEGEND

In the 1956 NBA Draft, the St. Louis Hawks picked Bill Russell No. 2 overall. However, they traded him to the Boston Celtics. Russell had also earned a spot on the US Olympic team. That year's Olympic Games overlapped with the beginning of the NBA season. Russell couldn't pass up the chance to compete

Russell led the US Olympic team in points scored. He averaged 14.1 points per game.

on the world stage. So, he headed to Melbourne, Australia, for the Olympics.

Team USA made it look easy. The team won every game by 30 points or more. Russell and his former college teammate K. C. Jones led the way. They crushed the Soviet Union 89–55 to win the gold medal.

Russell joined the Celtics in December 1956. It was well worth the wait. Russell had an outstanding rookie year with the team. He led the NBA with 19.6 rebounds per game. And the Celtics' 1957 title was just the beginning.

From 1959 to 1966, Boston won eight straight NBA championships. Russell

Wilt Chamberlain (13) was Russell's rival. Chamberlain led in most stats. But Russell won more games.

was the major reason for the **dynasty**. He earned the Most Valuable Player (MVP) Award five times as a Celtic.

Despite the team's incredible success, Russell was not always welcomed in Boston. Russell and his other Black teammates often faced discrimination. Parts of Boston had segregated housing. As a result, Black players struggled to

THE CIVIL RIGHTS MOVEMENT

Russell took an active part in the **civil rights movement**. In 1963, he went to the March on Washington. He joined Dr. Martin Luther King Jr. there. That year, Russell also led an **integrated** basketball camp in Mississippi. He stood up for other athlete activists as well. In 1967, boxing star Muhammad Ali refused to fight in the Vietnam War (1954–75). He was arrested as a result. Russell spoke out in support of him.

Russell (bottom left) supports Muhammad Ali (right of Russell) as he announces he won't fight in Vietnam.

find places to live. Restaurants and hotels also discriminated against the players.

In 1966, Russell started playing and coaching the Celtics at the same time. He was the first Black head coach in NBA history. As their coach, he led the Celtics to two more titles in 1968 and 1969.

6
12
21

CHAPTER 4

LARGE LEGACY

Bill Russell retired from basketball in 1969. He had spent 13 seasons with the Celtics. He'd earned All-Star honors in 12 of those seasons. During his career, he also led Boston to 11 NBA championships. To this day, no player has more championship rings.

Russell grabbed 21,620 career rebounds. Only Wilt Chamberlain had more.

In 1975, Russell was voted into the Basketball Hall of Fame. However, Russell did not attend the ceremony. He did not accept the ring, either. Russell didn't want to be the first Black player in the Hall of Fame. He knew others had come before him.

Russell never stopped working for justice off the court. The United States recognized that in 2011. Russell was awarded the Presidential Medal of Freedom. This is the nation's top award for a civilian. Russell also backed new social justice struggles. In the 2010s, for example, Russell supported the Black Lives Matter movement.

President Barack Obama (left) gives Russell the Presidential Medal of Freedom in 2011.

In 2019, Chuck Cooper was voted into the Basketball Hall of Fame. Cooper was the first Black player drafted by an

NBA team. In response, Russell finally accepted his own Hall of Fame ring.

Russell died on July 31, 2022. He was 88 years old. Soon after, his No. 6 jersey was retired across the entire NBA. That means no new players can wear his

BLACK ATHLETES ON STRIKE

In 1961, the Celtics had a game in Lexington, Kentucky. However, a restaurant refused to serve the team's Black players. In response, Russell led a **strike** of the game. The other Black players refused to play, too. Nearly 60 years later, NBA players did something similar. In 2020, the Milwaukee Bucks refused to compete in a playoff game. They were protesting police killings of Black people. Russell spoke in favor of the strike.

In 2009, the Finals MVP trophy was named for Russell. He presented it to Kevin Durant (right) in 2017.

number. It was the first number to be retired throughout the league.

Russell will always be remembered as being one of the greatest NBA players. More importantly, he was a true champion of equality for Black Americans.

BILL RUSSELL

- **Height:** 6 feet 10 inches (208 cm)
- **Weight:** 215 pounds (98 kg)
- **Born:** February 12, 1934
- **Died:** July 31, 2022
- **Birthplace:** Monroe, Louisiana
- **High school:** McClymonds (Oakland, California)
- **College:** University of San Francisco (1953–56)
- **Major achievements:** Olympic gold medal (1956); NBA champion (1957, 1959–66, 1968–69); NBA All-Star (1958–69); NBA MVP (1958, 1961–63, 1965); Basketball Hall of Fame (Player) (1975); Basketball Hall of Fame (Coach) (2021)

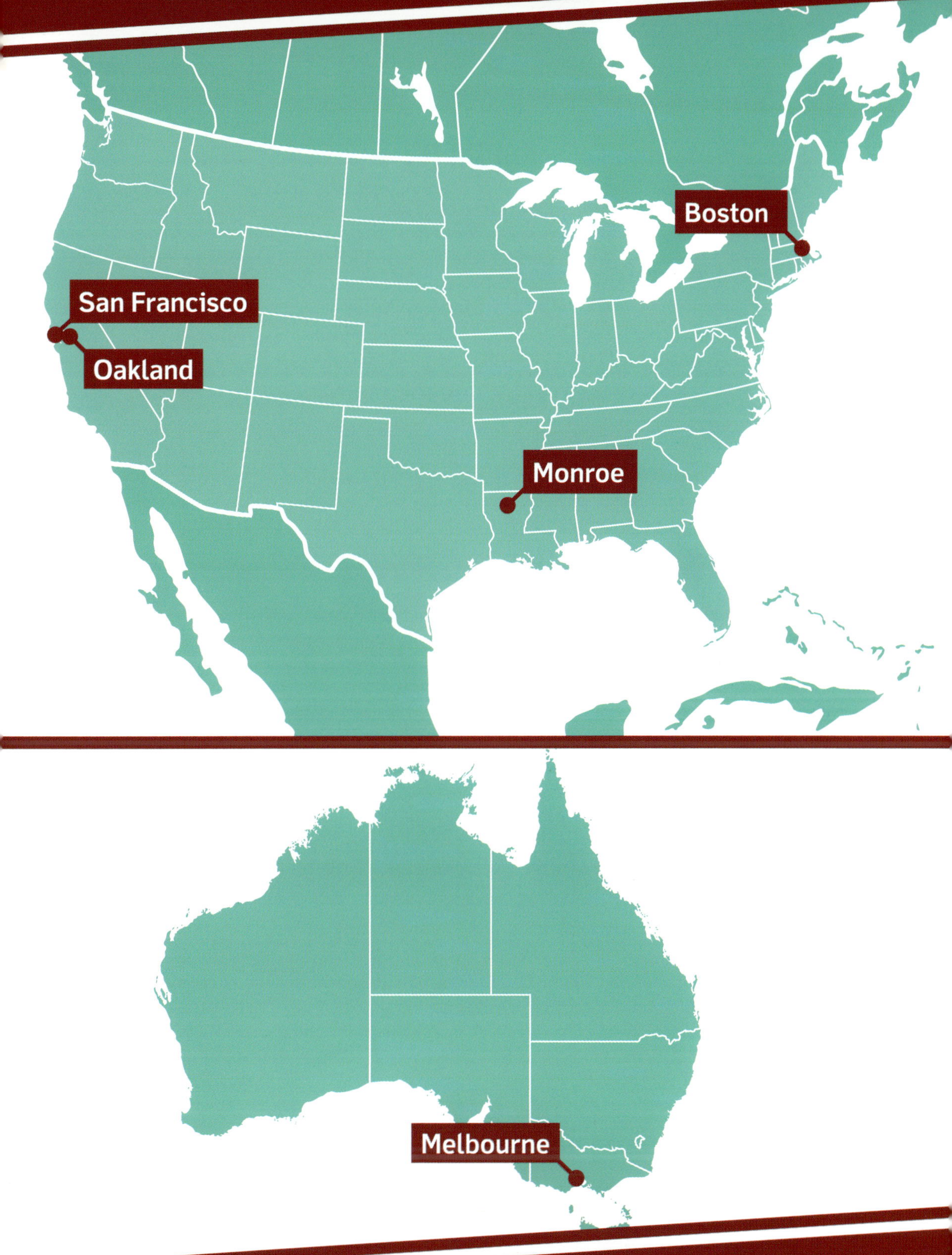
Boston
San Francisco
Oakland
Monroe
Melbourne

FOCUS ON
BILL RUSSELL

Write your answers on a separate piece of paper.

1. Write a paragraph explaining the main ideas of Chapter 4.
2. Do you think Bill Russell did the right thing when he didn't accept his Hall of Fame ring in 1975? Why or why not?
3. How many NBA championships did Bill Russell win with the Boston Celtics?
   A. 8
   B. 11
   C. 13
4. How can blocks help teams score?
   A. Defenders don't have much time to run to the other side of the court.
   B. Some blocks put the ball right in the hoop.
   C. The best shot blockers are also the best shooters.

Answer key on page 32.

GLOSSARY

chase-down block

When a player runs down the court and blocks a shot from behind.

civil rights movement

A mass struggle against racial discrimination in the United States in the 1950s and 1960s.

discrimination

Unfair treatment of others based on who they are or how they look.

dynasty

A team that has a long run of winning championships.

integrated

Including people of different races.

overtime

An extra period to determine a winner in a tie game.

rookie

A professional athlete in his or her first year.

segregated

Separate or set apart based on race, gender, or religion.

strike

When people stop working as a way to demand better working conditions or better pay.

TO LEARN MORE

BOOKS

Lowe, Alexander. *G.O.A.T. Basketball Centers.* Minneapolis: Lerner Publications, 2023.

Mahoney, Brian. *GOATs of Basketball*. Minneapolis: Abdo Publishing, 2022.

Whiting, Jim. *The Story of the Boston Celtics*. Mankato, MN: Creative Education, 2023.

NOTE TO EDUCATORS

Visit **www.focusreaders.com** to find lesson plans, activities, links, and other resources related to this title.

INDEX

Ali, Muhammad, 20

Basketball Hall of Fame, 24–26
Black Lives Matter, 24
Boston Celtics, 5–9, 17–21, 23, 26

civil rights movement, 20
Cooper, Chuck, 25–26

Great Migration, 11–12

Jones, K. C., 18

King, Martin Luther, Jr., 20

Melbourne, Australia, 18
Milwaukee Bucks, 26
Monroe, Louisiana, 11

NBA championship, 5–9, 18, 21, 23

Oakland, California, 11
Olympic Games, 17–18

Presidential Medal of Freedom, 24

St. Louis Hawks, 5–7, 17

University of San Francisco, 12–15

Answer Key: 1. Answers will vary; **2.** Answers will vary; **3.** B; **4.** A